COLUMBUS BLUE JACKETS

BY ETHAN OLSON

Book design by Maggie Villaume
Cover design by Maggie Villaume

Photographs ©: Jay LaPrete/AP Images, cover, 10–11, 15, 19; Dorn Byg/Cal Sport Media/ZUMA Wire/AP Images, 4–5, 7, 8; Chris Carlson/AP Images, 13; Tom Mihalek/AP Images, 16–17; Terry Gilliam/AP Images, 21, 23; Gene J. Puskar/AP Images, 24–25, 27; Nick Wass/AP Images, 29

Press Box Books, an imprint of Press Room Editions.

ISBN
978-1-63494-674-2 (library bound)
978-1-63494-698-8 (paperback)
978-1-63494-744-2 (epub)
978-1-63494-722-0 (hosted ebook)

Library of Congress Control Number: 2022919245

Distributed by North Star Editions, Inc.
2297 Waters Drive
Mendota Heights, MN 55120
www.northstareditions.com

Printed in the United States of America
Mankato, MN
082023

ABOUT THE AUTHOR

Ethan Olson is a sportswriter and editor based in Minneapolis.

TABLE OF
CONTENTS

1

The 2018–19 season marked just the fifth time the Blue Jackets had made the playoffs in their 18-year history.

IMPROBABLE
VICTORY

The Columbus Blue Jackets entered the National Hockey League (NHL) in 2000. It took them years to make it to the playoffs. Once they got there, they didn't have much success. By 2019, they had never won a playoff series.

Columbus had a chance to change that in the 2019 playoffs. The Blue Jackets faced the Tampa Bay Lightning in the opening round. No team had recorded as many points that season. That earned the Lightning the Presidents' Trophy. That trophy is given to the team with the most points in the regular season. The Lightning had 30 more points than the Blue Jackets that season. So it was a surprise when Columbus jumped to a 3–0 series lead.

Nearly 20,000 fans packed Nationwide Arena in Columbus for Game 4. They were desperate to see their team play in the second round. Center Alexandre Texier got the Blue Jackets off to a strong start. His wrist shot put Columbus up 1–0 less than three minutes into the game.

The Blue Jackets led 3–1 midway through the second period. But the Lightning fought back. Tampa Bay trailed

Sergei Bobrovsky makes one of his 30 saves in Game 4 against the Tampa Bay Lightning.

4–3 late in the period. Blue Jackets goalie Sergei Bobrovsky made sure his team kept its lead. With seconds left in the second period, the puck bounced off

Alexandre Texier celebrates his goal against the Tampa Bay Lightning in the 2019 playoffs.

the wall after a hard shot. It was headed toward the Columbus goal. Bobrovsky stuck out his left leg to stop the puck. That kept Columbus in front heading into the third period.

The Lightning needed at least one goal to tie the game. Still down 4–3, Tampa Bay pulled its goalie. It had three minutes left to save its season. Approximately one minute later, Columbus left winger Artemi Panarin scored on the empty net. Nationwide Arena erupted. The Blue Jackets went on to win 7–3. For the first time, Columbus fans were able to celebrate playoff success.

A RECORD-BREAKING OCCASION

The Presidents' Trophy was first awarded in 1986. Going into the 2019 playoffs, only six Presidents' Trophy winners had lost in the first round. And no team that had won it had ever been swept in the playoffs. The Blue Jackets' win over Tampa Bay changed that in 2019.

2

The Blue Jackets
played their
first game at
Nationwide
Arena on
October 7, 2000.

COMMUNITY
BUILDING

Any professional team is supposed to represent the community it's in. When Columbus needed a team name in 1997, it was up to the locals to decide. The team ran a "name the team" campaign. After receiving more than 14,000 entries, the decision came down to two names: the Blue Jackets and the Justice. The Blue Jackets won out. It honors the many Ohioans who fought for the Union during the US Civil War (1861–1865).

The Blue Jackets' NHL start was rocky. They finished last in the Central Division in their first season in 2000–01. Yet the Columbus community stayed behind them. Fans had shown up to watch the team's training camp before the season. An average of 17,500 people came through the gates during the regular season.

•TRAGEDY STRIKES

In 2002, tragedy struck Columbus. A deflected puck flew into the stands of Nationwide Arena and killed 13-year-old fan Brittanie Cecil. To recognize her life, the team wore small hearts with her initials, "BNC," on their helmets. This tragedy changed the entire NHL. The league required every team to add more netting behind the goals.

Tyler Wright checks an opponent into the boards during a January 2004 game.

The Blue Jackets closed out their first

season with a bang. An overtime goal

from center Tyler Wright saw them win

4–3 against the Chicago Blackhawks. The team was far from the playoff race. But Nationwide Arena was still packed. This only added to the excitement around the first-year team.

Fan interest grew further heading into the 2002–03 season. That was because of rookie Rick Nash. The Blue Jackets traded up to take Nash with the first overall pick in the 2002 draft. The powerful left winger made his NHL debut at 18 years old. He played well in his rookie season. But the Blue Jackets still finished last in their division.

Nash only got better, though. He scored a league-high 41 goals in his second season. The Blue Jackets

Rick Nash scores one of his 31 goals in 2005–06.

struggled again that year. But Columbus
had a star to build around for years
to come.

3

Ken Hitchcock
won 125 games in
four seasons as
the Blue Jackets'
head coach.

HELP FROM
HITCHCOCK

In 2005–06, Columbus pushed for its first playoff appearance. But the team was hit by injuries to its star players. Rick Nash and defenseman Rostislav Klesla each missed dozens of games.

Columbus made a change the next year. It hired Ken Hitchcock as its new head coach during the 2006–07 season. The team also moved on from its general manager. Columbus hoped new leadership could improve the team. Hitchcock knew what success looked like. He had coached the Dallas Stars to a Stanley Cup in 1999.

With Nash and Klesla healthy, the Blue Jackets had their best season yet in 2007–08. Better play from Nikolai Zherdev also helped. The winger had a tough start to his NHL career. But Hitchcock trusted him. Zherdev turned his career around in 2007–08. He finished with a career-high 61 points. But the Blue Jackets still missed the playoffs.

Team captain Adam Foote was traded in 2008. This opened the door for rising star Nash to lead the team in 2008–09. He was coming off a career-high 69 points.

Nikolai Zherdev celebrates a shootout goal in a 2007 game.

And he was ready to push Columbus into the playoffs.

With three games left in the regular season, the Blue Jackets were on the brink of the playoffs. One more win would get them there. They faced the Chicago Blackhawks on the road. After falling behind 2–0, the Blue Jackets rallied to send the game into overtime. They eventually won in a shootout. Columbus was on its way to the playoffs for the first time. In the first round of the playoffs,

COVER STAR

Rick Nash developed into one of the biggest names in the NHL in Columbus. In 2008, the Blue Jackets named him team captain. Heading into the 2008–09 season, his stardom was also recognized outside Columbus. The video game *NHL 2K9* featured Nash on its cover.

A Columbus fan makes a joke at the expense of Detroit Red Wings goalie Chris Osgood before a 2009 playoff game.

the Blue Jackets faced the defending champion Detroit Red Wings. Columbus scored five goals in Game 4. It wasn't enough. Detroit swept the Blue Jackets. But expectations grew for Columbus fans.

RICK NASH

The Blue Jackets loved Rick Nash before they even drafted him. They had the third pick in the 2002 NHL Draft. But they traded up to the first pick to make sure they could take the left winger. The move paid off. Nash wasted no time living up to expectations. He scored in his NHL debut, a 2–1 win against the Chicago Blackhawks. After the season, he was a finalist for the Calder Memorial Trophy. That award is given to the best rookie each season. A year later he became the youngest player in NHL history to lead the league in goals.

Nash led Columbus in goal scoring for eight of his nine seasons with the team. By the time Nash left Columbus in 2012, he had set many team records. As of 2022, he was still the Blue Jackets' all-time leader in games played, points, assists, and goals.

Rick Nash's No. 61 was
retired by the Blue Jackets
on March 5, 2022.

4

Matt Calvert had four points in six games during the 2014 playoffs.

INVADING
THE EAST

The Blue Jackets spent their first 12 years in the Western Conference. In 2013–14, they made the switch to the East. The Blue Jackets made the playoffs in their first year in the new Metropolitan Division. They matched up against the favored Pittsburgh Penguins.

Columbus lost Game 1. Then the Blue Jackets went down 3–1 in the first period of Game 2. Matt Calvert stepped up from there.

The winger scored in the second period to get Columbus back in the game. He then scored the game-winner in double overtime. The Blue Jackets had finally won their first playoff game. They added another overtime win in Game 4. But the Penguins went on to win the series.

The 2015–16 season started terribly. The team lost the first seven games of the season. Head coach Todd Richards was fired. He was replaced by John Tortorella. The new coach made an instant impact.

•STINGER

The Blue Jackets have had the same mascot since entering the league. It's a giant green insect named Stinger. It was designed to look like a yellow jacket. Stinger wears a Blue Jackets jersey and a Union cap. That honors the meaning behind the team's name.

John Tortorella was known for his fiery coaching style.

Tortorella's Blue Jackets broke multiple records in 2016–17. A 10–0 win against the Montreal Canadiens was the most goals scored for the Blue Jackets in a single game. Tortorella marked his 500th career win in a 4–3 overtime victory against the Vancouver Canucks. He was the first United States–born coach to reach that mark.

Columbus was consistently good under Tortorella. His defensive style made it hard to score against Columbus. In 2019, the Blue Jackets won their first playoff series. But the success didn't last. Stars like Artemi Panarin and Sergei Bobrovsky left after that season. The team needed something to excite its fans. It did that with a big move after the 2021–22 season. Columbus signed All-Star free agent Johnny Gaudreau. Fans hoped

Patrik Laine (29) led the Blue Jackets with seven game-winning goals in 2021–22.

"Johnny Hockey" could lead the team to more playoff success.

COLUMBUS BLUE JACKETS
QUICK STATS

TEAM HISTORY: Columbus Blue Jackets (2000–)

STANLEY CUP CHAMPIONSHIPS: 0

KEY COACHES:

- Ken Hitchcock (2006–10): 125 wins, 123 losses, 36 overtime losses

- Todd Richards (2012–16): 127 wins, 112 losses, 21 overtime losses

- John Tortorella (2015–21): 227 wins, 166 losses, 54 overtime losses

HOME ARENA: Nationwide Arena (Columbus, OH)

MOST CAREER POINTS: Rick Nash (547)

MOST CAREER GOALS: Rick Nash (289)

MOST CAREER ASSISTS: Rick Nash (258)

MOST CAREER SHUTOUTS: Sergei Bobrovsky (33)

Stats are accurate through the 2021–22 season.

GLOSSARY

ASSISTS
Passes, rebounds, or deflections that result in goals.

CAPTAIN
A team's leader.

DRAFT
An event that allows teams to choose new players coming into the league.

GENERAL MANAGER
The person in charge of a sports team, whose duties include signing and trading players.

OVERTIME
One or more extra periods played after regulation if a game is still tied.

ROOKIE
A first-year player.

SHOOTOUT
A tiebreaker used in the regular season if two teams are still tied after the three periods and overtime.

WRIST SHOT
A shot that involves the use of the wrist and forearm to push the puck forward.

TO LEARN MORE

BOOKS

Berglund, Bruce. *Big-Time Hockey Records*. North Mankato, MN: Capstone Press, 2022.

Doeden, Matt. *G.O.A.T. Hockey Teams*. Minneapolis: Lerner Publications, 2021.

Nicks, Erin. *NHL*. Minneapolis: Abdo Publishing, 2021.

MORE INFORMATION

To learn more about the Columbus Blue Jackets, go to **pressboxbooks.com/AllAccess**.

These links are routinely monitored and updated to provide the most current information available.

INDEX